It Ain't Rocket Science
A Common-Sense Guide to
Making IT Projects Work

IT AIN'T ROCKET SCIENCE
A COMMON-SENSE GUIDE TO
MAKING IT PROJECTS WORK

**HOW TO FIND AND FIX THE UNDERLYING PEOPLE,
PROCESS, AND BUSINESS PROBLEMS THAT CAUSE
THE MAJORITY OF TECHNICAL ISSUES**

Susan C. Cooper

Susan C. Cooper, Presage Publishing Company, Dallas, TX 75206

This book has been reviewed in its entirety by legal counsel.

Special thanks to Cindy Clayton for title assistance.

ISBN-13: 9781530232413
ISBN-10: 1530232414

Library of Congress Control Number: 2016903600
CreateSpace Independent Publishing Platform
North Charleston, South Carolina

CONTENTS

WHY I WROTE AN IT BOOK FOR NON-IT BUSINESS LEADERS

- Because "duh!" isn't a section on your weekly project template
- Because the sales guys may lose a commission if information technology (IT) consultants tell the truth
- Because nobody wants to talk about the elephant in the room
- Because your real problems aren't caused by your software
- Because people don't want to be told their baby is ugly, but if they've bought the pageant package, they should probably be gently told.
- Because if clients fixed these basic problems, we IT consultants wouldn't have a job (This is what we tell each other on our worst days, but I think we'd have a much better job if we could all move on and get your business running the way it should. Call me simple, but isn't that why we're all here?)

While you're reading, think about every single IT foul-up, snafu, mess, missed deadline, and major butterfingers moment you've had to deal with at every single company you've ever worked for, and tell me if I'm right that identifying and solving the real problems will help your software work better.

Why No One Tells the Truth in IT

In twenty-plus years in IT consulting, first as an independent IT business owner and then, for the past twelve years, as an IT consultant at one of the top tech companies in the world, I've noticed that my Fortune 500 and government clients have consistently had the same set of foreseeable issues over and over again. These nontechnical issues are people, process, and business problems, and they overshadow and block efforts to complete effective IT projects, implementations, and goals.

The most talented IT consultants are able to spot these non-technical road blockers, but our sales and management teams often tell us, "No one wants to be told their baby is ugly." They advise us to address what our clients *perceive* to be problems rather than the problems themselves. Problems caused by people, process, and business issues are surprisingly consistent throughout the Fortune 500, and we can address them if we're willing to talk about the elephant in the room.

Why the Humble IT Consultant Has a Unique and Undistorted View of Business, People, and Processes

The simple fact is that the people already employed by a company, while being able to identify some of these problems, aren't typically able to *solve* them because internal politics stand in their way. They also don't have the luxury of being able to think about the business's needs and processes independently of the personalities and alliances they quickly become embroiled in.

Outside business consultants initially have a better chance than employees at avoiding internal politics, but simply by arriving on-site, they start to become part of the corporate culture, even during the envisioning and interviewing stage, because they too must forge alliances and make backroom deals to try to push through some of the items on their agendas.

But because companies bring in IT consultants to look at something else entirely—namely, software—in many cases, we get to see things as they are. Why? Because although we're looking at software, the effectiveness of the software is completely dependent on how it's being used and who is using it. As IT consultants, we see how the company *actually* works and not just how the company is *supposed* to work. An IT consultant sees the unvarnished truth about how not only people, processes, and products impede the effectiveness of a specific piece of software but also how, in many cases, the mission of the company itself impedes the effectiveness of a specific piece of software. Since we aren't trying to sell anything, protect any political turf, or embarrass anyone, we are in the unique position to see what needs to be done and make recommendations.

I'm sick of hearing that if our clients knew what they were doing, we wouldn't have a job. Actually, we'd have a much better job because we could be doing the kind of work that really matters to a company instead of revisiting the same set of tired issues again and again. We really do want you to succeed.

People say technology changes quickly. It may, but the issues it's trying to solve have been the same since the beginning of... well, business.

Some things I'm going to propose are so simple and obvious that I'm almost embarrassed to write them down. But if people can build an empire out of giving other people groundbreaking advice like "Pay off your debt" and "Put your money in envelopes and budget that way," I figure I can point out the simple mistakes I see almost everywhere. These mistakes are easy to fix, yet people don't do it. They probably think that fixing things can't possibly be so easy when they've always had so much trouble fixing things before.

Money-Back Guarantee
I've been doing this a long time, and I think that at this point, I really must have seen it all. But just in case I haven't, I always welcome a good story. If you have encountered a failed IT project

or department that this book doesn't cover, please e-mail me at ITMgmtGirl(at)gmail.com, and I'll be happy to refund the purchase price of this book—after you share your story.

There are no quick fixes. Well, there are, but they don't involve buying any new software or getting someone to provide a vision in a PowerPoint slide deck. But they will work. Let's chat about them now.

What's In It for You?

You will reap many benefits when you address underlying issues that limit your success. Here are some of them:

- Easily identify (and fix) the self-defeating behaviors that consistently stymie your efforts to implement successful IT projects and operations.
- Get past reinventing the wheel in IT development, and start focusing again on your core business mission.
- Hire the best, and keep them happy.
- Identify what a great chief information officer (CIO) will look like to your business.
- Realize that there is no such thing as "being technical," and move forward with more confidence in your business and project capabilities.

The purpose of this book is to use humorous but true situations to do the following:

- Show how to ward off the most common, entirely preventable IT deployment problems by following three simple steps that most Fortune 500 companies ignore.
- Provide specific examples of the types of behavior and processes that cause the majority of technical issues, how to identify them, and what to do about them.

- Tell the truth about Fortune 500 companies, using humor and examples that resonate with CIOs, IT managers, and IT staff.

Demonstrate how IT leadership is fundamentally different from the typical chief "x" officer (CXO) function and why it requires a different kind of CXO than your typical "thought leader."

THE THREE IT DEPLOYMENT RULES YOUR COMPANY IS IGNORING RIGHT NOW

B Y *DEPLOYMENT*, I mean any IT-related change that is being foisted on your users, whether it's a network upgrade they may not be aware of or an upgrade to the software they most commonly use that makes your company money.

Any change can lead to an outage—sometimes because simultaneous, congruent changes occur, and sometimes because a newly installed product does not perform the way it was expected to. Sometimes people who are making the changes are not as well versed in their roles as they should be.

About businesses and their specialized needs in IT, I constantly hear, "But I'm special. I'm different. My business has never been done before in the history of the world." I hear this a lot—I mean a lot—but I have yet to run across a business that doesn't fall into three broad categories:

1. Manufacturing (e.g., autos, circuit boards, oil)
2. Services (e.g., spa, banking, transportation)
3. Retail (reselling what other people make)

A Basic Three-Step Deployment Process

All three of these business types should follow the same basic deployment process, which has three components. Let's look at these components in detail.

Know Thyself

Know what you're looking for. What do you want to get done each day? You'd be shocked by how many large companies wing it when it comes to major global software deployments.

When I've asked how they define a successful rollout, I've actually been told, "We're just going to see how it goes," and ostensibly from that statement, if it goes well, "We'll roll out *more*." And more is never defined.

Let me be clear in my advice: no.

At this point, when you're about to deploy a major change affecting the people who make money for your company, there had better not be any "we'll see" about it. You'd better know, as I do when I do these types of deployments. Trust me when I say that my boss's boss isn't about to find out that something unforeseen has happened before I find out. If you want to go the wing-it-and-see route, I'd suggest a career change into something that doesn't affect one hundred thousand computers at one time or a global multinational network or a secure infrastructure. Maybe you can do Internet marketing or something that will allow you to "see how it goes."

Here's an example of not knowing your business: I am told quite often, "We aren't sure what our metrics should be" on a deployment, and then they suggest that I should know. Metrics aren't a secret that's kept by some consultant somewhere; they are simply the quantitative measures that are most important to your business. Asking me about your metrics is like asking me how long a piece of string should be. It's your business—are you seriously telling me that you have no idea how to define success? Sure, I can offer modifiers and opinions based on my experience, but really and truly, the metrics are yours, and they come from the business. If you don't know what those are, see your chief executive officer (CEO)—and after that, you'll probably be seeing the door.

Think Globally but Act (at First) Locally

I am staggered at the number of times I've seen a global deployment of the widget software start globally. Seriously, folks, your entire IT infrastructure (or most of it) is based in the United

States, but you really think that deploying in Seoul first is the best course of action? I know you run a global business, but you want to think local first. You should always deploy to yourself, your boss, your help desk, your networking teams, and so on, first. In other words, IT eats its own dog food.

The benefit to this approach is that you will personally see what actually happens when the software is upgraded, and everyone around you will have a fairly strong opinion about it because they are IT folks too, and they'll be thinking about how to improve the user experience. You'll also get feedback from people around the water cooler who would never have bothered to say anything otherwise.

At the very least, your help desk (which, granted, may be in another country) should be part of the second deployment group. You want them to understand what your one hundred thousand or so end users are seeing when they call in. Simple, right? Yet probably 90 percent of the companies I consult with insist on starting their deployment overseas. The rules of deployment are simple: start locally (with you, your boss, your help desk, and your IT department), and then hit any department that is in the same building or on the same floor. That way, you'll once again get the water-cooler talk, and people will stop you on the way to the bathroom to either complain or compliment you on the job. If you're deploying overseas in Borneo, that isn't going to happen, and you certainly don't want to find out that the software isn't deploying very well once it's already installed halfway around the globe.

One Is the Loneliest (and Most Productive) Number
Although you'd think this next point would be obvious, I'd say 90 percent of companies don't even bother to check if the software actually got to where it was going. No, I am not making that up. They've typically outsourced it, and the outsourcer sends it out overnight and then goes home (remember, people in outsourcing countries typically don't work the long hours that Americans do). It's very rare that these things are tracked down and actually

checked. Sure, sometimes they'll keep an eye on the console or remotely monitor it, but many times, people never actually check (either by making a connection to the remote computers or by e-mailing or calling someone overseas) to make sure the software actually got there. Yes, although we work in a virtual, remote environment, what we do has physical, real-world implications for your end users (people who make you money) daily. Every day you check and make sure that the project is physically doing what you expected it to do. Did the software get to the targeted computers? Did it install? Does it work on the targeted computers? You must do these steps and spot-check your deployments every day. Simply looking at a management screen that shows that shows that software was theoretically sent out to a remote corner of the globe is a recipe for disaster. Multiple languages and platforms make things complicated, and just because the software deployed flawlessly in Australia doesn't mean it's hitting the European subcontinent with the same grace.

Yes, every day, review the previous day's deployment *by yourself* or with a very small team, if necessary. Then adjust the upcoming schedule slightly to account for the lessons learned and the feedback you've gotten. Sounds like the most obvious thing in the world, right?

The worst situation I've ever seen was one in which the project manager brought the entire team together to "talk through the project" on a call every day that lasted several hours. Every single day. Though years have passed since then, every time I drive by one of that company's stores, all I can think is *"Aargh!* I wasted years of my life sitting there in meetings doing nothing!" The logical part of my brain is still incensed at all the wasted time.

A good project manager should be seen in the actions of his or her team but not heard. As a great project manager, I always know where everyone is, what each person is doing, and what needs to be done next, and at a moment's notice I can substitute one action or person for another without breaking the synergy of the team. Managing a project of this magnitude is an art and a science, and it's absolutely never accomplished by committee, by constantly having people on the phone, or by being so clueless that you waste a couple of dozen folks' time by sitting on a call with them and asking questions like, "Uh…what's next?" What's next is that your boss needs to get someone to manage who knows what he or she is doing.

Cluelessness also manifests itself in people who call international meetings without an agenda. They ask you to provide training without telling you the point and ask you to "just put something together." They keep you on calls for more than fifteen minutes even when you aren't directly related to the issue at hand. On a technical project call, they start sentences with, "I'm not technical, but…" If you don't know what you're managing, then please don't announce it. (we already know.)

THERE'S NO SUCH THING AS BEING "TECHNICAL"

THE WORLD HAS changed since IT used to be a cost center under the chief financial officer (CFO). If you're paying the CIO anything approximating a CXO's salary (or really, if he even has the title), he should probably be able to talk the talk by understanding the technology he's tasked with overseeing. You wouldn't tolerate a CFO who can't create or read a complex financial analysis, so why would you hire a CIO who isn't "technical" enough to understand the underlying technology? The same goes for IT managers. If I hear one more person announce "I'm not technical, but..." once more on a technical call, I may have to write another book. Since when did announcing your lack of credibility in the field you are managing become a way to introduce yourself?

Also, while we're on the subject of CIOs, allow me to let you in on a little secret: The CIO doesn't need to be a visionary. He just needs to be able to ensure that the people who make the widgets can make the widgets faster and without IT slowing down the process along the way. That requires someone who can identify your business problems and find and implement the technology that solves those problems. That's it. Nothing else. How's that for a little B2B advice? That job requires a hardworking pragmatist, not someone who's building a legacy out of a data center in a cornfield.

I can almost guarantee that there is an inverse relationship between pie-in-the-sky CIO plans and basic things like, oh, data backups. And no, it's not what I would call uncommon at all, especially pre-9/11. Now we see it only about 50 percent of the time.

Oh, and by the way, there really is no such thing as being "technical." However, there is such a thing as having the ability to solve business problems using technology—and that's really what the IT business is about. You'll note that I put the word *technical* in quotation marks above because people use the word as a synonym for *smart* or *intelligent*, or they use it to mean "I read the manual, and you didn't," and the like. So before announcing that you know nothing about the field you're managing, please remember that anything related to IT is written in English, it solves business problems, and it isn't out there for its own sake. Understand what the heck you're managing, or keep your ignorance to yourself.

"Teamwork" and Other Time Wasters

S O LET'S SAY the widget software upgrade hasn't arrived on the manufacturing floor's computers during shift change. You're about fifteen minutes away from restarting the line and want to know why. Or maybe the widget software installed on all your corporate executives' desktops, but it wasn't supposed to. And the corporate executives certainly want to know why.

This is when someone like me is called in and given a quick rundown on what's happening and any troubleshooting steps that have already been tried. Then it's my job, as an IT consultant, to come up with a plan to further quantify and qualify where the problem is actually occurring. There's nothing worse than spending an hour reviewing logs and seeing no hint of the problem the client has asked about because the client sent me to the wrong region of the world; the issue is really happening in Detroit, not Dubai.

I'll typically join an ongoing bridge call with the client. One thing I've noted is that on most technical troubleshooting calls I'm on, one or two people are actively trying to solve the problem, whereas two dozen others—well, they are simply there. In addition to me and my main technical contact, we'll also have my contact's coworkers, his manager, in many cases his manager's manager, the project manager, and typically most of the global network and telecom staff sitting around listening in on the line. After that, pretty much anyone randomly found in the hallway or on instant messenger (IM) who may or may not have anything whatsoever to do with the outage is brought in.

This motley crew is assembled because someone, somewhere, thinks there may be an chance that we will suddenly need the network guys in Tokyo for a workstation problem in Papua, New Guinea, and we want to be sure they're sitting right there on the call already—never mind the fact that we could call or IM them at will.

But here's the thing: one of the really cool parts about a technical job is that you can, in many cases, ask me a question that includes only the most basic bits of data, and I'll be able to answer the question. Sometimes I will ask for some background, and no matter how long the problem has been going on, it should take the customer less than a minute to tell me. I really don't need to have been on the call for the past four hours listening to the network guys troubleshoot the router. If I had a question about the router, I'd simply ask the question, the network guys would answer, and we'd be done. Precision questioning is why my company is paying me an absolute minimum of $150,000 a year and why my company is charging you no less than $500,000 a year for my services.

However, consultants who are on a call at your behest when the call isn't something they need to be on are probably doing two things: first, they're working on something else in the background entirely unrelated to your issue, and second, they're quite happily billing you the entire time while they tune you out.

Twenty extra people at $250 an hour (a fairly common billing rate) equals a lot of wasted money ($5,000 for you purists).

I can already hear some of you saying, "Five thousand dollars! That's nothing to make sure we have the right people on the call. We think of it as insurance." It actually isn't. You don't have the right people, the people you do have are wasting their time, and no one is paying any attention anyway. If you don't believe me, take a poll to see how many people can tell you what you just said. I know, I know—I'll never make it in middle management unless I sit in meetings all day. That's just fine with me because I have real work to do—work I actually enjoy. And I will enjoy it less if it involves wasting my time.

I will very rarely take a meeting, and that's because I don't need to talk to you. If I have a question, I'll ask you, and that will be it. I don't need to "open a conference call" so that your manager and your manager's manager have something to do. If you don't know what's going on, read the e-mail I sent you, or pick up the phone and call me.

True story: At a major bank, an IT consultant was recently told that if a missing IT charge wasn't at least a million dollars, the CIO thought it wasn't worth his time to track it down. I'd say that's a group of people who are wasting some serious money. Think it doesn't apply here? Five thousand dollars an hour becomes a million dollars in two hundred short hours. I suspect that most of us sit in on a lot more than two hundred hours of calls we don't need to sit in on. I have personally spent probably close to two decades on calls during which two dozen people were billing for their time and providing absolutely nothing of significance.

Takeaway: The right person in the right job knows the situation, the problem, and the players, and that person can get it done much faster than two dozen people who are sitting in on the call only half-listening and who are working on their real problems in the background. Groupthink is extremely limiting and can be downright detrimental,[1] if you believe the *Harvard Business Review*. Leave your smart people alone, and let them do their jobs.

In the South, we have a saying: You can say anything you want about a person as long as you start the sentence with "bless your heart." So bless your heart, but stop wasting everyone's time and racking up tens of thousands of dollars in consulting fees to have technical folks on the call who honestly don't need to be there.

Let the technical person handle the technical problem. A technical problem becomes more difficult (and expensive) to solve when two dozen people are sitting in on a call listening to the troubleshooter breathe.

---

1 Willaim Schiano and Joseph W. Weiss, "Y2K All Over Again: How Groupthink Permeates IS and Compromises Security," *Harvard Business Review,* March 15, 2006, https://hbr.org/product /y2k-all-over-again-how-groupthink-permeates-is-and-compromises-security/BH188-PDF-ENG.

MAD-LIBBING YOUR WAY THROUGH AN IN-HOUSE ARCHITECTURE, ALSO KNOWN AS REMAKING A PRODUCT IN THINE OWN IMAGE

REMEMBER THOSE OLD Mad-Lib pads? You had your friend give you a random noun or a verb while you filled in a silly story, and once you read the story aloud, it sounded ridiculous. The story I'm going to tell sounds ridiculous too, but it will also sound way too familiar if you've spent any time in IT.

A client might say to a consultant:

"Your product is OK, but I love the other competing software product

- that was discontinued
- that was something we developed in-house
- that is eight versions old
- that is a competitor's"

The client then says:

"But I was forced to buy your product instead

- by my supervisors
- because of my budget
- because the other product no longer exists [could this be a clue, perhaps?]

- because I was bowled over by the sales girl
- because your product was free to me, bundled with a lot of other products"

The client then says:

"So I'm going to

- demand that you change the product I just bought to match the old/discontinued/competitor's project
- internally either reprogram your product or write a wrapper or other interface around it so it's used in a way that is completely different from the way it's intended to be used [This takes the form of changing the interface so much that it is no longer possible to leverage people's previous experience with the publicly released product, and everyone has to be retrained to use it]
- reprogram around the product so much that I lose all ability to track using the built-in, internal mechanisms of the product; as a result, I also lose the ability to hold anyone accountable for issues because I can't track anything
- use only 10 percent of the product, and use many other products that I think are better as stopgaps in place of the suite I just bought—these additional products, are, of course, from multiple vendors and require their own end-user training
- threaten your engineering and consulting staff by telling them that if they don't make your product work in the image of the old product, I'll stop using your product and rip it out, thereby sending your sales staff into freak-out mode"

This is typically at least 50 percent of what I spend my day trying to derail. And I don't even get a sales commission; I just want the damn thing to work.

Bless your heart: I know it can and will work, and if you'd just get out of my way, we could really make some progress.

The Plane Doesn't Know Who's Flying It

A NEIGHBOR OF mine is a fighter-pilot instructor. One night at a neighborhood party, one of my less enlightened friends asked him if he had trained any female pilots.

"A few," he answered.

"Wow, that would be so weird," my friend said, sounding exactly the way you're imagining. "I don't think I'd want a woman flying me around in a plane."

The fighter-pilot instructor looked at him and, without missing a beat, said, "Well, the plane doesn't know it's a woman flying it."

Enough said.

Technology doesn't know or care who's programming it or troubleshooting it; if it's working, the person doing the job is doing a fantastic job, regardless of gender. If such sensible views were the real measure of things, there would be a lot more women in IT.

Remember Edward Snowden? He's the former CIA employee who in 2013 copied classified US National Security Agency information without permission and gave it to journalists. One of the major complaints I've heard about the veracity of Snowden's claims is that he was a college (and high school) dropout who didn't have a degree in computer science, so how could he possibly have been making six figures in an IT job? Easy—he was a white male in his late twenties to early thirties, and in IT that's about all you need to get your foot in the door. Well, to be blunt, that and being about twenty pounds overweight will get you a place in the next hiring wave.

Think I'm kidding? Go visit a Fortune 500 tech company's parking lot sometime. Laments from human resources (HR) people saying they can't find any qualified women in IT[2] are ridiculous for several reasons. The first is that if most men met the technical requirements women have to meet to get hired, companies would have the same problem of not being able to find enough qualified men.

Most of the male consultants I know do not have a bachelor's degree and usually don't have any experience beyond what they've gained at the technical consulting firm that employs them. Most of the consultants I know who are women—well, both of them—have master's degrees in their field and ten to twenty years of experience in the real world before they even walk in the door as a consultant.

Even Sheryl Sandberg, chief operating officer of Facebook, says the lack of diversity in companies is "pretty depressing."[3] She pointed out that the world is "still overwhelmingly run by men" and noted that less than 6 percent of CEO positions at top companies worldwide are held by women. In her view, we have "a leadership problem."[4]

According to a recent *USA Today* analysis of employment documents from Facebook, Google, and Yahoo, in 2014 leading technology companies in still underemployed minorities in addition to women, in both technical and nontechnical positions. The data showed that African Americans and Hispanics made up only 5 percent of these companies' workforce, compared to 14 percent nationally.[5]

---

2 Sherrell Dorsey, "Need to Remove Racial Bias in Hiring for Tech Jobs? There's an App for That," *The Root,* March 14, 2016, http://www.theroot.com/articles/culture/2016/03 /need_to_remove_racial_bias_in_hiring_for_tech_jobs_there_s_an_app_for_that.html?wpisrc=topstories.

3 Laura Petrecca, "Sandberg: Lack of Diversity in Firms 'Pretty Depressing,'" *USA Today,* August 15, 2014, http://www.usatoday.com/story/tech/2014/06/18 / sheryl-sandberg-tech-diversity-depressing-cannes-france/10760591/.

4 Ibid.

5 Davey Alba, "Microsoft Releases More Diversity Stats, and They Aren't Pretty," *Wired,* January 5, 2015, http://www.wired.com/2015/01/microsoft-diversity/.

It's the same story concerning gender. Facebook's tech sector is 85 percent men and 15 percent women.[6]

A mere 10 percent of Twitter's high-paying jobs, such as computer programming and other tech positions, are held by women.[7]

VMware Inc. reports that women make up only 19 percent of its engineers.[8]

In 2015, Microsoft's technical workforce was 16.9 percent women, a level that was basically stagnant or .02 percent lower than its published 2014 levels.[9]

As is the case in other tech companies, the gender gulf widens at the management level. Microsoft's management is largely white and male: 88 percent of the company's executives are male, 12 percent are female; 81 percent are white, 20 percent are Asian, 3 percent are Hispanic/Latino, and 1 percent are black.[10]

In 2014, Microsoft CEO Satya Nadella had to "walk back comments he made at a women's computer science conference [] when he suggested women don't need to ask for a raise—they should just trust the system."[11] Trust in a system that can't even seem to hire me? I don't think so.

6 Sandra Drake, "Facebook Releases Diversity Numbers: Senior Level Employees are 74 Percent (or More) White, Male," *San Francisco Business Times*, June 25, 2014, http://www.bizjournals.com/sanfrancisco /bizwomen/news/latest-news/2014/06/facebook-releases-diversity-numbers-senior-level.html.

7 "Twitter Is Very White and Male, Company Diversity Figures Show," *San Francisco Business Times*, July 24, 2014, http://www.bizjournals.com/sanfrancisco/ blog/2014/07 /twitter-white-male-company-diversity-yahoo-google.html.

8 Peter Burrows, "VMware Diversity Data Show More Women in Technical Jobs," *Bloomberg Business*, July 29, 2014, http://www.bloomberg.com/news/articles/2014-07-29 /vmware-diversity-data-show-more-women-in-technical-jobs.

9 "Our Employee Community," Microsoft workforce demographics, last modified September 30, 2015, https://www.microsoft.com/en-us/diversity/inside-microsoft/default.aspx#epgDivFocusArea.

10 Alba, "Microsoft Releases More Diversity Stats, and They Aren't Pretty"

11 Laura Mandaro, "Microsoft's Nadella Does About-Face on Women and Raises," *USA Today*, October 14, 2014, http://www.usatoday.com/story/tech/2014/10/09/nadella-women-raises/16999381/.

Even Pinterest, which is a female-focused search engine, still has men dominating their positions in tech (79 percent), engineering (81 percent) and leadership (84 percent). The imbalance isn't only a matter of gender. Pinterest's leadership is exclusively 90 percent white or Asian.[12]

In response to this kind of situation and in an attempt to change the way tech companies screen their employees, Stephanie Lampkin, who happens to be a black woman, developed Blendoor, a blind recruiting app that helps tech companies hire on merit alone, taking both gender and race out of the equation.[13] Lampkin developed the app because she felt frustrated by not being taken seriously in the tech industry despite having an engineering degree from Stanford and an MBA from MIT Sloan.[14]

And although companies make half-hearted stabs at "diversity" I can't tell you the number of times I attended a "diversity" meeting in which I was the only female engineer—there weren't any other female engineers to attend. So who did male business leaders bring in to counsel us on how to be successful women? Administrative assistants (I highly respect the amazing job they did at those meetings, but this wasn't what I was looking for) and one out-of-town female manager. I mean, you can't make this stuff up.

In one meeting that included myself and two other female engineers (three female engineers out of thousands of male employees set the record for my "diverse" engineering team experiences during my entire twelve-year tenure), a male leader actually asked me with a straight face if I was interested in going into

---

12 Jessica Guynn, "Exclusive: Pinterest Launches Innovative Diversity Project," *USA Today,* July 30, 2015, http://www.usatoday.com/story/tech/2015/07/30/pinterest-diversity-women-underrepresented-minorities-silicon-valley-jesse-jackson/30881091/.

13 "Race Matters: Black Woman Develops Hiring App for Tech Companies That Eliminates Bias," *Bossip,* March 14, 2016, http://bossip.com/1292622/race-matters-black-women-develops-hiring-app-for-tech-companies-that-eliminates-bias/?.

14 Dorsey, "Need to Remove Racial Bias in Hiring for Tech Jobs? There's an App for That"

sales. I doubt he asked this of male engineers who seemed to climb the corporate ladder effortlessly. And why would I go into sales? I knew from past experience that I could make a ton of money in IT if given the chance.

But surely this pattern of under-employment of women and people of color is finally being addressed now in 2016. I mean, they are working on diversifying tech? I found this article from a decade ago (2006) and sadly, at least in Microsoft's case their diversity numbers are either getting worse or staying very flat. The percentage of women in executive ranks actually fell from fifteen percent in 2006 to twelve percent in 2016. That doesn't sound like much of an improvement. My favorite quote regarding why Microsoft hasn't been able to make much progress on the diversity front comes from one of the few women to occupy the executive rank, former HR Executive Lisa Brummel: "In our 20+ years of committed efforts toward managing diversity and inclusion effectively, what we've learned is that diversity is not a finite goal that can simply be achieved, then "checked off" a list; it is a journey that requires constant self-assessment and recommitment."[15]

Call me crazy but in order to actually become a more diverse company, you need to *hire more women and people of color.* Not talk about it. Not come up with sound bites that are basically excuses. Not put up another website talking how diverse you really want the company to be. But actually hire people who are diverse. They are out there. I promise. And if you don't think so, I can find them for you.

As a highly technical female, I was asked to interview other candidates only twice in my entire twelve-year career: once, within the first three months of being hired, and then again a couple of years ago under a new manager, who was unfortunately later fired (for something unrelated). Except for those two times, no one ever approached me about interviewing, although I would hear

15 http://www.cnet.com/news/microsoft-releases-diversity-stats-says-much-work-still-to-be-done/ Microsoft releases diversity stats, says 'much work' still to be done. Oct 2, 2014. Web.

through the grapevine that my male coworkers, even the newly hired ones, were interviewing. Why? I can only surmise that our male managers felt more comfortable approaching junior male engineers to do the hiring instead of senior female engineers. Whatever the reason none of the senior females or engineers of color is hardly ever approached to interview.

And one thing I do know that like hires like: if a bunch of early-thirtyish, non-bachelor-degreed white guys who are twenty pounds overweight are hiring and doing the interviewing, they'll basically hire themselves again and again.

Why Root Cause Doesn't Matter

K IDS CONSTANTLY ASK why. For example, "Why is the sky blue?"

You could tell them that it just is. Or you could tell them that technically the sky is blue because blue light, consisting of shorter and smaller waves that are easily seen, is scattered more than other colors. But the net sum is still the same: the sky is blue.

And remember how annoying it is when kids keep asking why? *Why* doesn't really matter in this case. What is just is.

IT is a bit like that. You can waste tons of money on the following:

- The whys (a.k.a. root causes)
- The what ifs (a.k.a. bugs)

Let's talk about why the whys and what ifs, which are incredible time wasters.

It's been trendy during the last decade or so to look for root causes, and this seems to make sense in the world of computing. If we find out the underlying cause, we can fix it. And if IT were still in the land of ones and zeros, that would be a great idea. Except IT is not.

Root cause matters only if it's reproducible and something we're *likely to see again*. What do I mean by that? With the network, the firmware, the hardware, the software, and the billions of files that have to be just so to make your infrastructure work, there are many chances for someone to screw something up. Maybe a program gets upgraded over the weekend, and the upgrade process was flawed; for example, someone didn't reboot when he or she should have. That means your upgrade isn't complete, and the system isn't in a state of readiness. Maybe a file gets accidentally overwritten by another version from another program; maybe a file gets deleted. Maybe a service pack that is critical hasn't yet been applied, and you're seeing what we commonly refer to as bugs.

None of this is really reproducible, and spending hours—or, more likely, days or weeks—tracking down the root cause is a waste of time. Seriously, if we know that reapplying the service pack fixed the problem, should we really try to reproduce the problem so that we know which file was accidentally overwritten? Does it matter? In a perfect world where everything is tracked, finding out root cause is a great idea. It would be interesting (and not much else) to see which file caused which problem, but the simple fact is that there is so much churn on a daily basis that what you see wrong on one server is very rarely going to be the same thing that's wrong on another server.

And, to be blunt, if you were so organized that you could track the problem down to the file level, you probably wouldn't be screwing up to start with.

By the way, as an English major, I have to point out that *root cause* is redundant—the word *cause* by definition refers to the *root* of something. Think about it.

Now we'll visit the what ifs (a.k.a. bugs).

First, I have to break it to you: just finding something that doesn't work the way you think it should doesn't mean there's a bug or, even if there is a bug, that the bug is going to be fixed.

Why? Well, let's look at an example in the world of color wavelengths or what we commonly refer to as light:

- White is all colors (or wavelengths) combined.
- Black is the absence of any color (or wavelength.)

Does this make sense? Not to me, no matter how many times I tried it myself in middle school art class when our teacher gave us a color wheel to spin and the colors disappeared into white.

Is this a bug? No, although it defies our expectations of how something should work.

So how does this apply to the IT world?

Let's say your job is to deploy software. You have the following settings throughout your product that you can choose in any combination:

- Reboot only if a user is logged on.
- Reboot only if a user is not logged on.
- Reboot whether or not a user is logged on.
- Reboot servers always.
- Reboot servers never.
- Reboot workstations always.
- Reboot workstations never.
- Show a five-minute countdown timer before reboot.
- Allow the user to put off the reboot for one day.
- Allow the user to install the software at any time.
- Allow the user to install the software only during a maintenance window.

Let's say you choose these two options:

- Show a five-minute countdown timer before reboot.
- Reboot only if a user is logged on.
- Allow the user to install the software at any time before the deadline

When these two options are set, let's say we send out the newest version of an accounting software to your workstation. After it is installed, you get a five-minute countdown timer, and your workstation reboots. Makes sense, right?

Now we add one more setting: allow the user to install the software at any time. So we now have these three settings:

- Show a five-minute countdown timer before reboot.
- Reboot only if a user is logged on.
- Allow the user to install the software at any time before the deadline
- And then a new, additional setting: Force the software to install if it has not been installed by a certain date.

The predetermined date rolls around (and it happens to be a workday), and the software automatically begins to install without any input from the user although it does notify the user that it is installing. Then it immediately reboots (skipping the countdown timer), thereby surprising the end user. The user calls the help desk to complain (because this user is an executive), and you, the IT consultant, get hauled in front of an executive committee to explain what happened.

Bug, right? Not really. And here's why it's not.

In this case, hitting the deadline overrode the fact that the user wasn't logged in, and the software (which needs a reboot to finish installing anyway) just forcibly rebooted.

The software installation was forced when the deadline was reached, so if we looked in the code, we would see that there are no niceties to bother with, like a five-minute countdown before reboot. Although things didn't appear to work the way you thought they should, if you were to open a bug case with the software company, the software company would say that the software is working the way it was intended to.

You may not agree, and just as the fact that all colors (wavengths) of light mixed together equal white doesn't make sense to me, what happened may not make sense to you, but technically what happened is not the result of a bug. So save yourself a lot of time and money: test every repercussion you can think of that your users might encounter. Do this in a lab. If you find something that you really think is a bug, bring it up. But if we tell you there's a reason for it, don't beat it to death. It's only going to waste your time and money. I have worked with people who really get hung up on this type of thing and just want the software to follow the same logic of notifying the user (even with slightly different settings). But due to the complexity of available options, it may sometimes act in an unexpected way. Not a bad or broken way, just unexpected. If it's 'unexpected' doesn't that mean it doesn't work correctly? Not on the code level it doesn't. Yes, it may confuse our expectations but if it follows the underlying code, the fact that it did not notify the user to reboot is not a bug. So save yourself some billable time by testing in advance so you know how things are going to work.

Software today is incredibly complex; there are often thousands of settings and dozens of independent software products at play that the main product you're working with depends on. So, sometimes it's not possible to know without testing how a system with a particular set of settings is going to respond. That's why we have you, the well paid IT employee to figure that out. It's also why we need these folks to be smart and capable. This process of documenting everything (while nice for a competent person to do a quick review of) does nothing if the person running your IT infrastructure has no idea what they are doing behind that document. And many don't. Why? Usually the people hiring them (managers and sometimes other technical staff) are clueless as well. Honestly, I don't think 80% of IT staff could pass a logic test, much less a test on the software that they supposedly manage.

Why You Don't Need to Know If It's Corporate Sabotage

HERE'S A REALLY easy rule: if someone costs your company *avoidable downtime*, fire that person.

I know: I'm such a meanie. But firing someone under those circumstances really isn't mean; it's expected. Trust me, the people causing the downtime fully expect to be fired and may even be relieved because they will now be free to reevaluate their lives and go do something they are good at. And I'm not talking about small mistakes; I'm talking about egregious, gut-churning, you-couldn't-have-made-up-something-so-insanely-bad-in-your-head kind of mistakes.

Active Directory is where things like your company user name and password are stored. It also contains information about what groups you are in, software and files you have access to, and so on. Obviously, it's important if it allows you to log in to your work computer in the morning. However, if someone deletes *sysvol* (the part of the Active Directory that keeps track of your login accounts), find out who it was, and fire him or her. You think I jest and that this is just a ridiculous, made-up example? No, I've seen it happen, and the person didn't get fired because no single person was held responsible for anything (just a group), and there was no tracking in place. Two days later, it happened again (true story). All because someone needed more room on the servers. I know: I can't stop laughing about it either, and I saw this a decade ago.

Of course, the plan to create more space by deleting *sysvol* worked for about fifteen minutes, until all of the deleted accounts started getting replicated around the world as expected...and then people were unable to log in because their accounts no longer existed. Oops.

Here's another example of egregiously bad judgment (bless their hearts): I was sitting at a laptop my customer had given me. I had direct access to the customer's network (i.e., they were too lazy to actually get me logs to troubleshoot with, so I had to go get them myself).

Then, all of a sudden, VIPSoftware 2010 started to install. Normally, this would be a good thing; software installation is common in my job. Except I knew for a fact that VIPSoftware 2014 had previously been installed on that laptop. So I strongly suspected that downgrading to the previous version was probably not what was wanted. After a few hours of trying to reach the help desk in Kuala Lumpur, I finally reached someone in the United States who told me that yes, someone in Kuala Lumpur had accidentally deployed the old VIPSoftware on top of the new one. Mind you, that person had deployed it to every single computer on their global network and had then gone home for the day. We got it stopped eventually, but as you can imagine, it takes a while to pull back that sort of thing. The only reason the company wasn't more affected is that its base of operations was in the United States, where it was around 9:00 p.m. (EST), and most employees' computers were turned off.

So if someone does something that causes entirely avoidable downtime, fire that person. If you have an unexpected outage, track it down to see who did it. And if you don't know how to do that, you definitely need to up your hiring standards.

The simple fact is that the rest of your (competent) staff who had to spend all night fixing these entirely preventable issues (and your staff knows this too) will be relieved you have a handle on it and understand the issue, and they will be happy that you're sending a message that insanely dreadful judgment won't be tolerated. People who make these kinds of egregious mistakes rarely get fired, and I haven't figured out why. I honestly think it's because their management has no idea how hard it is for these people to make such mistakes in the first place. Ignoring the mistakes and looking the other way requires essentially having no security in place, no procedures in place, no tracking in place, and no accountability in place, and then allowing someone who apparently doesn't have the slightest idea about his or her job to have unfettered access to it all. Way to go.

These examples aren't examples of sabotage per se but of sloppiness that results from having unnecessary customized tools in place between the doer and the original software, not tracking anything, not having the right person in the job, and having no one truly responsible for anything—oh, and don't forget farming it out overseas. But really, except for those major mistakes, the problem could have been avoided entirely. See how simple it is?

Action item: if you can't tell if it's corporate sabotage or plain old stupidity, it really doesn't matter.

I Think You Meant to Ask This of Your Magic 8- Ball

H ERE'S A TYPICAL e-mail I might receive from a Fortune 100 company that is paying me an exorbitant amount of money to help its managers and/or staff:

Subject: Problem with Blob Software
Hey, our Blob Software is looking funny. Here's a piece from the log:
02.02.2012. BlobLogisnotrunning. Blah blah blah.

And that's it. No context. No information about where this is happening, no supporting or related logs, of which there are usually well over two dozen (or even hundreds) for most products. I don't even get the rest of the log that the snippet came from. I'm always tempted to reply with a cryptic "Ask again later," because I have about as much ability as a magic eight ball to solve the problem when so little information is given to me.

Here's how troubleshooting works (take notes): I listen to every single thing you tell me, and I listen to what you think it is, what your boss thinks it is, and what the last consultant you had look at it thinks it is. I listen to all of the unrelated issues you bring up that you've run into before that you think it is. I even listen to what you don't think it is. And here's where the magic comes in. I then disregard everything you've told me, and I ask for data:

logs, event viewers, more logs, dumps, analysis, and so on. I ask for many other things that may appear to you to have little relevance. I cross-reference dozens of log findings that may or may not support the original hypothesis you gave me or what I thought was the problem five minutes ago. I do this because sometimes I find that the problem you're seeing is a secondary or even a tertiary one, and the underlying cause has to do with a component that seems to be completely unrelated. I liken this to unraveling a web. I also do this because if I'm already down there, in the weeds, looking around, I might as well let you know about everything I can see.

But what I have to have, what I must have, is information. So please don't withhold information, thinking that withholding information makes you look smarter or that I should be able to solve the problem without the data. I really can't. In spite of what the sales guy may have told you when he sold you my special abilities at $250 an hour, I don't possess any special powers that you and your staff don't already have. However, what I do have is a willingness to spend many hours, even many days, slogging through bits and pieces of logs and seemingly unrelated pieces of information trying to find out why your Blob Software is "acting kind of funny," as you say. And yes, it does take everything I have some days to not immediately reply and ask, "Is it wearing a clown nose, or what?"

So please, send me everything I ask for—every log, every scrap of information—get as much detail as you can. Withholding information doesn't make you look smarter to your boss when you say, "See how long it took our consultant to solve it!" Withholding information simply ensures that you are billed every time I have to ask for the same set of logs.

IF IT VIOLATES THE LAWS OF PHYSICS...

H ERE'S A CONVERSATION I've had more than once:

Employer: "So, one problem that we're really stumped about is how to protect this one guy [and it's always one guy] who spends eleven months a year on the African coastline, walking along the shore and taking samples [true story, by the way]. He never dials in, and he never gets e-mail; he just does water analysis and uploads all his results via fax machine, or sometimes he e-mails us once a month."

Me: "Does he have any Internet access at all?"

Employer: "No."

Me: "Well...if he's not on the network and doesn't have Internet access, he's probably not going to need much updating at all, is he?"

I say this to my client in the most supportive and least threatening way possible without sounding like I'm trying to be supportive or nonthreatening. Actually, about 70 percent of my job is trying to nudge people in the right direction in a nonthreatening way. I try to give them the feeling that they came up with the idea themselves. I am 30 percent technical engineer and 70 percent therapist, it seems.

A request for help may also contain phrases like these:

- "One of our ships goes out for nine months at a time…"
- "In the desert with no communication devices…"
- "In the oil fields…"
- "On secret assignment…"

But the gist is always the same—it's someone whom management can't figure out how to update because he is never on the network. Well, if he's never on the network, he's probably not going to be downloading anything you need to be concerned about.

Other versions of violating the laws of physics include the following:

- "I have a really slow network and can't figure out why I can't copy large amounts of data all at once, so I need you to come fix your software."
- "We are running out of disk space, but we aren't going to buy any more disk space, and we want you to fix that."

And yes, I've been known to say, "Well, we're kind of trying to violate the laws of physics here…"

I let them finish that thought.

Outsourcing: Hey, Let's Take Everything That's Important to Us and Give It to a Stranger (in Another Country!)

E VEN THOUGH OUTSOURCING has become the defacto
standard, let's talk about the various forms it can take and
why that may not be the greatest idea since sliced bread.

Offshore Outsourcing
American companies taking their Intellectual Property (IP) and
transferring it to the farthest corners of the globe is concerning
for several reasons. First, when it comes right down to it, IP is just
about the only thing that most companies have that has any innate,
reproducible, transferable value. Sure, there may be physical stock
for retailers which can encompass anything from planes to t-shirts,
but it's mostly a company's intellectual property that makes the
company who they are; everything from their branding to their
network schematics to customer data.

And I'm just thinking out loud here, but giving IP to an offshore outsourcer; someone you don't know and very likely isn't
subject to the United States laws should your data be sold, exposed,
corrupted or lost might be a tad iffy even under the best of circumstances. And don't count on security or encryption to avoid
this; it's becoming an almost everyday occurrence for the largest
companies in the world to have data breaches on a global scale

bleeding everything from user credit card data to embarrassing personal information on web sites. The correlation between all of these information breaches and the fact that most data is now handled by non-Americans isn't causal but it's certainly concerning.

In addition, as one of our commonly used outsourcing countries Brazil has recently shown us, there can be enormous political, socio-economic, and other factors like weak controls that may result in inadequate privacy regulations. Serious strategic risks may also be at play as different country laws may not protect something as basic to Americans as "trade secrets." Offshoring your IP basically becomes an expensive exercise (this time with lawyers instead of paying your IT staff a decent wage) in becoming an expert on the country where your data resides.

I'm obviously not an expert in foreign offshoring law, but these are basic questions I've always had that I have never received a solid answer on.

The Cloud

Let's just talk about the Cloud briefly. What is it? Your company's data gets stored in typically one of three scenarios: physically on-premise ("private cloud"), with the hosting company ("public cloud") or a mix of the two ("hybrid"). In all three cases it is managed by an outsourcer or outside company.

Here are some things I would keep in mind; whether they apply in your case or not depends on how much money you have to spend on the service and how flexible the cloud provider is willing to be:

1. In the case of a hybrid or mixed cloud environment you've outsourced your company's IP to either a foreign or domestic entity (depending on how deep your company's pockets are). Your company's IP is basically on the internet (for all practical purposes). You may or may not know where the data is physically or even virtually located. The data may be moved around at will by the hosting

company.[16] It can (in a lot of cases) be moved (or backed up) to other countries. In a shared hosting environment, your company data will share space with other companies' data. Making it vulnerable to attacks their software and data may suffer as well. Your company's IP, of course as with all outsourcer scenarios, will be managed by people you don't know and couldn't pick out of a police line-up if you had to.

2. Oh and about your data...did I mention that it may *technically* be the outsourcers data now? Many times the outsourcer will take ownership of the data because it's in their legal best interest in case there's data loss to decrease their liability. That's nifty for them, but what about for your company? Is that really what you want to do? Put your data, online, with someone you can't see, don't know and who now owns your data? There may be legitimate reasons that this scenario works for your company. But I'd be very clear on what they are before signing up.

3. In many cases (though not all, again it depends typically on how much clout you can wield. Read: money spent) the outsourcer can mine it for almost anything including opportunities to sell your company even more services. It's a well-known fact that at least a dozen of the largest ISPs in the United States routinely scan stored files for alleged child pornography. When they find it, they're obligated by federal law to blow the whistle.[17] And yes, child porn is repugnant and should be reported, but the point is that there's probably less privacy than you believe.

---

16 we may transfer to, store, or process Customer Data in any country where we or our Affiliates or subcontractors have facilities used to provide or support the Services. https://azure.microsoft.com/en-us/support/legal/subscription-agreement-nov-2014/ Web. November 2014.

17 When is your data not your data? When it's in the cloud. http://www.info-world.com/article/2613756/cloud-storage/when-is-your-data-not-your-data-when-it-s-in-the-cloud.html March 2013. Web.

4. Many times, your company is wholly responsible for configuring your Applications in the cloud to ensure adequate security, protection, and backup of customer data.[18] Which, to me, begs the question of why you are doing the heavy upfront work if it's a hosted solution.

When in Doubt, Bring Them Out

Some companies prefer to bring foreign workers to the United States en masse rather than hire American workers. If you were to hang out at a top telecom company's parking lots in states from Texas to Florida, you would find yourself in what felt like little India every morning. Easily 50-60% of the staff (I'd call them employees, but technically they aren't) is an Indian national on an H1-B visa.

I physically saw this myself in 2004. I called someone who is still familiar with this Telecom and he confirmed that this situation still exists. Twelve years later. And this is just a run of the mill Fortune 500 we're talking about. They certainly aren't doing any rocket science. The programs they implement and troubleshoot are garden variety off the shelf IT apps that anyone can go take a week long class in to get familiar with. Any decent well paid IT consultant should be able to easily meet this standard.

What's interesting about the outsourcing approach is that the hiring wages for these out-of-country workers are in most cases, exactly the same as American wages[19]. At this particular telecom, I

---

18 https://azure.microsoft.com/en-us/support/legal/subscription-agreement-nov-2014/. November 2014. Web.

19 The requirement to pay prevailing wages as a minimum is true of most employment based visa programs involving the Department of Labor. In addition, the H-1B, H-1B1, and E-3 programs require the employer to pay the prevailing wage or the actual wage paid by the employer to workers with similar skills and qualifications, whichever is higher. https://www.foreignlaborcert.doleta.gov/pwscreens.cfm

United States Department of Labor Employment and Training Division. Foreign Labor Certification. February 25, 2016.

sat next to the IT recruiter on the floor, a woman who ran the HR desk. I remember very clearly, in 2006, hearing that the company paid Indian foreign nationals with a bachelor's degree annual salaries of $65,000 ($78,000 in 2016). It paid Indian foreign nationals with a master's degree annual salaries of $80,000 ($96,000 in today's dollars). Apparently, where the degree came from was irrelevant. And yes, that isn't a lot of money, but it's certainly enough to hire Americans.

But the company doesn't hire very many Americans. Why? I've noticed that it works its Indian workers 24/7 for the three years they are here—the company seems to have carte blanche to work them as long and as hard as it wants to. Each year, this telecom company also holds a company-wide ceremony when it hires one or two (out of thousands) of these workers as full-time employees. In general, these people are very bright and incredibly hardworking, but they certainly don't have the special knowledge about the IT field—knowledge of financial calendars, of how end users think and react to software deployments, and of unspoken rules about American business—that an American has.

This example is by no means a one-off. If you spend any time at all in Middle America at one of the biggest retailers, you'll notice its corporate headquarters in IT has become predominately Indian as well.

And forget the argument that the differentiating factor here is the IT degree: it's not. I have a BA in English, and most of my former male counterparts at one of the world's top software companies did not earn a college degree at all. The one person I know who did earned his in marine biology. Some IT employees do end up earning their IT degrees once they have the six figure job, but I can assure you that the top tech companies hire on ability, not on schools or résumés (or at least not in the jobs where the rubber meets the road.) I'm sure there's an entire prestige university thing going on in the management ranks that I know nothing about that disadvantages those who put themselves through four years of undergraduate studies at a state school without taking a single loan or receiving a single grant. (Although my school wasn't fancy, between the premed courses and the literature, history, biology, and music classes I took, I got an unparalleled education.)

An American company entrusting its data to foreign nationals is also something to think about. Remember: it's information first, technology second. Don't forget why you and your company are even here.

Speaking of measures that don't make a whole lot of sense: I've found that the same clients who turn off networking on their workstations for security reasons (thereby completely blowing the entire point of a computer) also seem to be the ones who send their work product overseas.

When I say it like that, it doesn't seem like such a great idea, does it? I don't care if you're paying $1.85 an hour or not. Think I'm being dramatic? Consider the primary motivators for out-of-country outsourcing:

1. The company wants to control cost (it's less a matter of schedule and quality). But people at the majority of companies will say that they aren't satisfied with their ability to measure even their gains; they don't have the tools to keep a proper scorecard. Think about this before outsourcing. In any measure.

2. How much does outsourcing really save a company? It saves companies approximately 20 percent of one-quarter of the IT spending pie, resulting in 5 percent savings in the IT budget. For a million-dollar IT budget, that's $50,000, or one really bad employee, in common-sense terms. And of course, the offset is that productivity, quality, and scheduling efficiency drop, which results in a net loss of revenue, the opposite of what you were hoping for in the cost-savings department, eh?

3. At the end of the day, people in a majority of companies simply believe that they've chosen the wrong vendor and decide to switch vendors. It probably doesn't occur to them that outsourcing is the problem. Not the outsourcer!

4. Worker productivity: another unanticipated effect of outsourcing, besides the spectacularly bad customer service that we've all grown used to, is that workers in other countries have protections that we, as Americans, don't. For instance, a typical American worker, while charging you the equivalent of $130,000 per year, is going to work his or her ass off. Americans have no job protection and no overtime protection, and no minimum rest periods are required. I can attest to this after having worked with many global companies. I would stay on the phone for twenty-four hours but would be passed to different technicians in India and then Germany before being passed back to the United States to finish my troubleshooting. For whatever reason, I was expected to work nonstop while my overseas counterparts had a definite stopping point.

5. The typical European, Brazilian, and Indian enjoys a bevy of worker protections. For example, EU law says workers should work no more than forty-eight hours per week. Workers have the right to eleven hours of rest per day and one break for every six hours of work. Workers are guaranteed at least one full day off each week and paid leave for at least four weeks a year. Additional time off is given to night workers and those in particular fields, such as transportation. The Brazilian Labor Law prescribes an annual vacation of thirty days per twelve months of work in two parts (one that must be at least twenty days in duration).

I also found out the hard way when I was in Germany a day early to set up a classroom that Germans don't work on Sundays. The US workforce has none of these protections. The result is that Americans work harder, and we have one of the highest rates of productivity in the world.

To be blunt, we also have skin in the game when it comes to protecting American interests. Why an American company would send its data overseas to non-US Nationals (or worse yet, bring non-US Nationals to America) but pay them the *legally required* American wage is beyond me.

Actually, I do know. Corporations are playing the long game. Bringing in a glut of lower paying overseas workforce dilutes the salaries of American workers over the long term. This is clearly seen in why IT wages are not increasing even with inflation. If there was such a shortage of IT workers wages should have spiked or at the very least kept up with inflation; instead they fell.

Even since 2010 the average wage for American IT Skilled workers (or computer systems analysts) has gone from $39.28 per hour to $39.76 per hour. Or a total increase of just $4,000 in almost ten years. To keep pace with inflation a worker making 37.64 per hour (2007) would need to make 43.04 per hour in 2016. And right now they make $39.76 per hour. So wages for skilled IT workers have actually fallen.

But America's technology leadership is not, in fact, endangered. According to the economist Richard B. Freeman, the United States, with just 5 percent of the world's population, employs a third of its high-tech researchers, accounts for 40 percent of its research and development, and publishes over a third of its science and engineering articles. And a marked new crop of billion-dollar high-tech companies has sprung up in Silicon Valley recently, without the help of an expanded guest-worker program.[20]

But almost 90 percent of the Chinese students who earn science and technology doctorates in America stay here; the number is only slightly lower for Indians. If they're talented enough to get a job here, they're already almost guaranteed a visa.[21]

---

20 http://www.nytimes.com/2013/02/08/opinion/americas-genius-glut. html?_r=1 New York Times. February 8 2013. Web. A version of this op-ed appears in print on February 8, 2013, on page A27 of the New York edition with the headline: America's Genius Glut.

21 http://www.nytimes.com/2013/02/08/opinion/americas-genius-glut. html?_r=1 New York Times. February 8 2013. Web. A version of this op-ed appears in print on February 8, 2013, on page A27 of the New York edition with the headline: America's Genius Glut.

If anything, we have too many high-tech workers: more than nine million people have degrees in a science, technology, engineering or math field, but only about three million have a job in one. That's largely because pay levels don't reward their skills. Salaries in computer- and math-related fields for workers with a college degree rose only 4.5 percent between 2000 and 2011. If these skills are so valuable and in such short supply, salaries should at least keep pace with the tech companies' profits, which have exploded.[22]

According to Ross Eisenbrey the vice president of the Economic Policy Institute: "If there is no shortage of high-tech workers, why would companies be pushing for more? Simple: workers under the H-1B program aren't like domestic workers — because they have to be sponsored by an employer, they are more or less [in] indentured [servitude], tied to their job and whatever wage the employer decides to give them.[23]

The point of this section is to remind you that if you can get good at hiring the right IT folks, you can have everything you need at a much lower price point than outsourcing. And with a larger safety net. To be blunt the issue is that the people doing the hiring don't have the skills to hire the right person for the job.

And the US definitely has the personnel; they may not all be white, overweight middle class 30-something year old males, but they are women, men and women of color who don't fit the stereotypical mold that are currently being passed by for these positions. The talent is already here in the US.

And that is much more fixable than our current outsourcing system.

---

22 http://www.nytimes.com/2013/02/08/opinion/americas-genius-glut.html?_r=1 New York Times. February 8 2013. Web. A version of this op-ed appears in print on February 8, 2013, on page A27 of the New York edition with the headline: America's Genius Glut.

23 http://www.nytimes.com/2013/02/08/opinion/americas-genius-glut.html?_r=1 New York Times. February 8 2013. Web. A version of this op-ed appears in print on February 8, 2013, on page A27 of the New York edition with the headline: America's Genius Glut.

Your computers and network are only as secure as your worst employee. If a hacker can compromise a desktop they can get a lot of information. If they can compromise an employee; they can be unstoppable.

IF YOU'D BE AFRAID OF THEM IN A DARK ALLEY...

Do I need to finish this sentence?

Note: I have referred only to males in this section because of the extremely low number of women in any technical roles, including technical sales. As you've read in the section titled "The Plane Doesn't Know Who's Flying It," females in tech roles (even in sales) at almost every tech company are a dismal 10 to 19 percent of the people in tech roles. If instead of referring only to *he* in this section, I also referred to *she*, it would be incredibly obvious to everyone who had worked with me on those accounts whom I was referring to. There would be only one or two possibilities. My intent here is to help you navigate the crazies, not instigate them.

It took me a long time to figure out office politics—I mean a long time—yet figuring things out I've never seen before is my specialty. (Believe it or not, there's no special school you can go to or training you can get that will show you how to fix everything—or even anything—that the Fortune 100 and government can dish up, so you have to figure it out. In real time. Usually on a phone call with people listening to you breathe.)

Almost everything has been easier for me to figure out than office politics. That took me twenty years to figure out.

If you're logical thinker like me, and if you like to work at work as I do, you'll probably understand this explanation.

There are only two types of people in Fortune 500 companies:

- People who do the work that affects the bottom line
- People who don't typically interact with the customer

The people who do the work that affects the bottom line are the peons, the bean counters, the nerds, the geeks, and the Dudley Do-Rights of the world. They think they are making a bottom-line difference for their companies; they work hard at their jobs and in most cases, they genuinely enjoy their jobs. These can be front-line people who work retail cash registers or answer calls from large government agencies about how to best implement software. Their job is to sell, sell, sell—through every interaction they have with customers. Their job is to solve problems so their companies can sell even more. Kind of important, right?

The people who don't typically interact with the customer don't provide any kind of billable income. If they were good enough, they could be (in the case of a software company) frontline folks who could solve problems. But they end up being glorified secretaries who, in my experience, have the title of manager and get to approve my expense reports. But these people obviously need something else to do. So they make it up, to be honest. They do things like change the entire reporting structure above your head or create and collapse fiefdoms or change the name of what you do while not actually changing what you do. And of course, all of this renaming means absolutely nothing to the peons at the bottom who make the money for the company. After all, the frontline people aren't dealing with theory; they're dealing with the real world and know what their customers want. They don't have to come up with a new name for the help desk (such as the "answer desk"). They're the folks who get things done.

As you can imagine, the folks who aren't as productive and who spend time approving expense reports or creating schedules or reviewing surveys (snore) are going to need to have some way to make an impact. In my experience, they aren't able to do the actual work directly, but they certainly do seem able to insert themselves into it. This is where the entire world of office politics is born—from these people needing something to do. And because they don't have billable skills, they do other, more colorful things like throw fits, scream, berate people, and just generally lose emotional control more often than not. They range from simple crybabies to true sociopaths who are incredibly pesky and difficult to shake. You will lose almost every time a sociopath comes after you simply because a sociopath's rules are different. Here is my experience with these folks and some suggestions on how to handle them.

The manager screaming on the phone isn't getting great results because he's threatening or cursing; he's getting results because people working for him honestly want to do an excellent job, and anyone in his role who wasn't a total jackass would be getting better results. What he is doing, however, is causing preventable delays in a project. How? He's stressing out his people. He's causing missed work time. He's causing people to work more slowly and make more mistakes. He's making people regret working for the company. I can promise you that the people working for him are spending about 20 percent of their time wishing they were somewhere else and happily billing you for their time. What is that saying? People leave managers, not companies.

Behavior like his usually goes hand in hand with sitting in meetings all day. Why? Because people like him would have nothing else to do if they weren't sitting on a phone call or in a meeting or threatening someone. This isn't managing; it's being a psychopath without the scary music. Even behavior that doesn't warrant a forty-eight-hour psych-ward commitment qualifies as psychopathic if it doesn't pass the proportional response test.

Here's an example. I was teaching in Europe, and our account manager had tagged along. Sitting in the back of my classroom while I taught, he was ostensibly there to help me. The day before, he had been sick and out of the office. We took a coffee break. When we got to the front of the coffee line, our client offered to pay for my coffee. It was very nice but also not unexpected, because I had purchased coffee for the client the day before, when the account manager was out. I thought nothing of the client's buying me coffee and returned to teaching. The account manager returned to sitting at the back of the room (his version of doing something).

About an hour into teaching my class, I pulled up a copy of a very dramatic and long e-mail from the account manager to my boss (the account manager had written it while he was sitting in my class, mind you) explaining that I had violated the gifts policy with our corporate client. You get the idea—these people take something that is true, like my buying the client a cup of coffee, and put the most ridiculous spin on it.

I was teaching Monday through Thursday of that particular week, and the Account Manager had suggested earlier in the week that we go sightseeing on Friday. I have to admit that after the tumultuous week I'd already had with him, I was relieved when he called me on Friday morning to tell me that he was (once again) ill and that I should go out to enjoy myself, which is what I did. But when I returned to the hotel, I found that he'd e-mailed my manager (once again) to tell him that I had skipped an important client meeting (which had been set up after I left the hotel).

A few days after that, he simply stopped speaking to me. I went out one morning to meet him to take a taxi to the client's office, and my small talk went unanswered. The next two days while we were in London, he did not speak to me at all—not in answer to a direct question or anything, even when we were around the client. I have no idea if the client noticed, but it was truly odd. He flew out a couple of days early to "see his private physician" in the United States, as he put it in e-mail, because he was constantly on the verge of dying from something that, for some reason, I could never remember the name of. Sometimes I look him up just to see if he's still around. He is, but his illnesses seem to be getting more and more dramatic. He's also mastered the art of the gofundme account while maintaining a half-million-dollar home.

Customers, of course, can be guilty of the holier-than-thou attitude as well—to their detriment. I once sent out a standard annual meeting request for a thirty-minute "touch base" to one of my client's managers, whom we charge roughly half a million dollars per year for my services. This manager, who had been with our team for only about two months, is directly in charge of the type of work we do.

I asked when he might be available to meet with me. I was excited to tell him all the ways the company could cut my hours by changing a few simple things on its side. Instead of replying to me directly by making me the only person on the "To:" line and instead of ignoring my e-mail completely, he replied indirectly by moving me to the "cc:" line and adding his manager, our internal sales staff, and three of his comanagers on totally unrelated projects. Apparently, I had violated this commandment: "Thou shalt not approach the middle manager." My punishment? To be embarrassed mercilessly via e-mail.

Here's the actual e-mail he sent: "I'm not trying to be rude to Susan, but I do not have a clue why I need to talk to her or anyone about the subject item. Bob1/Bob2/Bob3, if you can explain to me why I should care, that would be great."

Now, the particular people he copied didn't have anything to do with my contract, so he wasn't going to get an answer out of them. And I had been relegated to third-person status, so it was obvious that he wasn't about to deign to reply directly to little old me.

This manager was new to the team, and perhaps he didn't understand how our vendor relationships worked. The particular corporate culture at this company rewarded bullying, so perhaps he had seen his higher-ups do what he did to me. Or perhaps he really had no idea why he should meet with someone who billed his company half a million dollars a year in entirely preventable costs, which I would have loved to discuss with him. Let's be serious, though—he was just an asshole. Because he could be.

Remember my telling you about the time a Fortune 100 company accidentally sent out an old version of software to all 180,000 of its desktops overnight? Well, when it happened, I saw it happen because it hit a laptop I had that the company insisted I use, so the laptop was subject to the same experience as end users' laptops.

I thought, "That's not good," when I saw the old version of the VIPSoftware hit my laptop. I didn't know they'd sent it to the globe, but the possibility did enter my mind. I simply closed my laptop. It was the evening, and I had no commitment to stop them from doing something stupid (after all, that's why they paid the folks in Kuala Lumpur). My job was to troubleshoot what they asked me to look at Monday through Friday from 8:00 a.m. until 5:00 p.m., or whenever they contacted me during evenings or weekends. It wasn't uncommon to be contacted then. However, in this case, no one contacted me, so I went to bed.

Of course, the next day, as soon as the company set up a marathon conference call to discuss hitting almost 200,000 desktops with an old version of VIPSoftware, I was the biggest help in the world. Pretty entertaining, especially when they realized it was their own help desk's fault. I have never heard so much backpedaling in my life about who was to blame for something.

Sometimes, bad or psychopathic behavior isn't as apparent as yelling or writing a truly odd e-mail response. I've had plenty of heavy breathers who surreptitiously joined conference calls without announcing themselves and who even refused to announce themselves after being repeatedly asked, "Who just joined?" We know seventeen folks are now on the call, but only sixteen have announced themselves. These people lie in wait until just the right moment to pounce on something innocuous said by an unsuspecting speaker. By joining unannounced and then jumping in unannounced, they force others to acknowledge their different status, and they usually manage the element of surprise so well that they can hijack the conversation.

I suspect that they listen in just to hear if someone says anything bad about them. No matter their motivation, you can identify them because you're always left with the feeling that you've been ambushed with no warning. Remember, if you'd hate to meet this person in a dark alley, he is probably not the best person to manage your people.

Here's another oldie but goody from one of my corporate clients whom I'll call the VIP Company: I was sitting in my home office but working on my customer's corporate network with both their corporate e-mail and IM on. So although I was a vendor, I had a VIP Company e-mail address, a VIP Company IM, a VIP Company laptop…you get the picture. I could not be more visible on their internal corporate network.

I was just working away when I got a call from our internal head of sales: "Hey, Susan, Bob (the customer) says he can't reach you, and he's escalated it up our internal chain."

No matter how you play something like this, you still look like an idiot.

I mean, do you bother stating the obvious? "Well, I'm sitting here at my desk, answering my phone (as you can see), on IM (in fact, I can see that the gaslighter is also on IM), and I haven't gotten a single communication from Bob." I would sound as if I wasn't quite sure, because of course I would be feeling completely perplexed about how this could have happened. If you are a technical person as I am, you double-check all your connections and make sure you really are on the network. It's only later in the day that you realize you were set up. Why? It's all part of the game; the customer has now required me to be even more responsive and to bend over backward to show how available and responsive I am. Why did he do it? Because he could. And from that point on, no matter when he calls, I get to answer the phone, and no matter what crazy thing he asks, I have to try to accommodate it. I must say, well played.

I don't think I'm speaking out of turn when I say that his employees kept a horrible little kewpie doll with pink hair in their offices on their shelves. When I asked them what it was for, they pulled up a picture of him on their e-mail system, and I must admit, without the pink hair, it was a dead ringer for him. I guess those without power still make do.

Once I was on-site in Detroit teaching three different classes, which meant I needed to load three different images on the training machines at the company. This is a given when going on-site to a client location to teach a class; we take a computer image that has all the software we need set up on it and load it on computers in the training class. So that students can do labs and troubleshoot in real time. My account manager offered to bring in help to set up the computer images. I repeatedly declined because each image copy would take only about ten minutes. I had taken three drives, and there were only twenty or so computers in the class. However, he still insisted that bringing in help might be a good way for me to get to know our internal, on-site staff.

After going in early the first day to load the images, a process that consisted of moving the drives from computer to computer and then watching the image copy, I hung out and ate some donuts with the other local consultants who had come in early, ostensibly help me.

After a long day of teaching, I logged in to my e-mail to find—what else—an e-mail from the account manager to my boss explaining that he had had to call in our local staff to bail me out and help load images that morning.

As you can see, these are not normal people in any sense of the word. Get as far away from them as you can. I truly don't think there's a way to win with these folks. Because their accusations contain just the barest nugget of truth, the fact that you have to explain it away makes you look guilty. Or incompetent. Even though it's not fair and it's not true, that's how life is sometimes. I wish I had a better way to thwart this type of attack, but I've fallen for it every time, as I don't really know how to tell anything but the truth (which in the long run is so much easier anyway).

Action item: fire them. If you can't fire them, at least put them where they can do the least harm—away from people. And projects. And processes. *Get them away from anyone you want to get anything done.* In fact, put them in the department you like the least. Put them together and stir. These people aren't like you and me. They're crazy. And unless you plan to earn a PhD in human behavior, I'd get as far away from them as you can. In my experience, there is no way to right that ship. They are nuts and are best handled from a safe distance.

You Get What You Pay For

I 'VE ALWAYS FOUND that it's easier and better to pay some-one a decent salary of $120,000 per year to pretty much save your bacon consistently than it is to pay three people $50,000 per year. A $50,000 person might as well be nobody for all the good you're going to get out of him or her.

The IT person you pay $130,000 a year (and it should never, ever, ever be less than this) is going to be smart enough and work hard enough to get things done. This is the guy or gal whom you want to have at your back when the icing hits the cake around the globe.

Unlike the globe-trotting CIO, this is the person who's going to get you and your company out of a pickle. Let me let you in on a little secret: The best IT people aren't told what to do; they know. And they keep a lot of crap at bay by dealing with it before you even know about it. They also steer you away from a lot of really bad decisions but still make you feel as if you made those deci-sions. See? Everyone wins.

Most IT folks are happiest when their systems are function-ing flawlessly, and their systems can't be happy if other people are mucking them up. A good, decently paid IT person will save your ass on a daily basis, and in most cases, you'll never know. So you can imagine (but threaten or cajole all you want)—we're typically going to do what we need to do anyway.

Show IT people some respect. One company I worked for routinely sent its IT consultants (who brought home between $150,000 and $200,000 per year) to an in-house technical conference that the company glowingly referred to as "geek ready." That's just great. I don't mean to make fun of you making fun of my job, but might I ask the middle managers whom I bill nearly half a million dollars a year if their way of paying homage to my incredible billing prowess is to lovingly call me a name I haven't heard since junior high?

Let me let you in on a little secret: I'm not a geek; I'm a professional. I advise the largest, most diverse, and most technologically savvy companies in the world on how to fundamentally improve their administration, security, and efficacy. I do this while charging you only one-fourth of what I bill.

You wouldn't send your accountants or financial officers to a "bean-counter" conference, would you? Show some respect. The only reason I can come up with to explain why it's OK to use a pejorative term to refer to someone who bills more than half a million dollars a year is that it keeps us down professionally. We might make $250,000 a year pretty handily at the top, but certainly no one is going to respect us for it. Or even guess that's what our take-home is.

IT professionals also have to be right—not in a marketing, this-may-work-in-a-few-years kind of way—but in an absolute, 100 percent, rock-solid-with-a-million-moving-pieces kind of way—every second of the day.

So, show some respect, why don't you?

It Ain't Rocket Science: A Checklist

ADMIT IT: YOU'VE been searching for this. A checklist! Aha! Something you can actually use! And share! So here goes. It comes with examples of some other destructive, counterintuitive situations I've run across. If you recognize yourself or your company in any of these examples, it's time for a little tough love. Bless your heart.

- Time to grow up! When I hear requests from a client like "We don't want to take the training class, but can you stand behind us and tell us how to click on the screen and walk us through how to use the software?" I want to run screaming from the meeting. Terrifyingly, this happens more than you think. I've found that charging someone $10,000 a day will usually nip this in the bud. Haven't had any takers so far. And yes, I've had to do this once, years ago. It was so distasteful, that even at $1,000 a day (my rate in the late 1990s) I refused to do it ever again. If you seriously can't be bothered to learn a new program or attend a class, this is not the business you should be in.
- KISS (Keep It Simple—you know the rest). Whenever someone asks me an incredibly complex question, the first thing I always ask back is, "What are you really trying to do?" I usually find that in most complex situations, people are trying to fit a round peg into a square hole, and if we can

just talk about the underlying problem, it's going to be a lot easier to solve than the one they just managed to dream up.

- Never share administrative accounts. For example, Bob and Sue are both admins at their company. They log in with the same administrator account and password. The same account. Stop! This happens a lot in incredibly large corporations, and there's no reason it has to happen. Setting up a unique admin account for every single admin user should be the most basic thing you will ever do. Why companies allow users to share accounts is beyond me, because there is no way to track malfeasance if more than one person is using an account.

- Always track everything—and I do mean everything: who makes what changes, who deletes which files, who adds which files, and who accesses and reads those files. Everything. And review it, not just when someone does something spectacularly bad, but every day. You should have at least one person devoted to tracking all changes and becoming familiar with the garden-variety changes made to your network and accounts every day. Especially the mundane changes. In well-run companies, it's not unusual at all for me to be asked the next day why I added someone to a group. "Because they need that access to do their job" is a legitimate answer.

- Stop following the crowd. IT is really, really simple. Data need to be accurate, available, secure and backed up. That's it. And if you're thinking, well, what about user design, user interfaces, marketing, blah, blah, blah?—that's either the chief technology officer's or chief marketing officer's job, and I don't comment on that separate skill set here.

- Hold people (not groups) accountable. If you're making any change on the network, on users' computers, in a database, or somewhere else, that change (which of course you are tracking and which of course has gone through a fairly stringent change-management process) should be tied to an individual's name—his or her name—not "the networking group" or what have you. If you hold people accountable (and I mean individually accountable) and do not get on the phone for an eight-hour rant at the group in general, it will get done.

Here's a review of the major topics in this book in a very simple format. If you haven't read the book, you'll have no idea what I'm talking about.

- Know thyself.
- What number of successful installs in a deployment defines success for you? (By the way, it will not be 100 percent, so just get over that). Write down that number. Go see if you did it.
- Think globally but act (at first) locally.
- Always eat your own dogfood first.
- One is the loneliest (and most productive) number, and that's the title of a song! So stop wasting everyone's time and review deployments daily by yourself.
- There's no such thing as being "technical." It's in English. Read it. If you can't, you are in the wrong job.
- Teamwork is a time waster.
- Don't give sociopaths a "job" by allowing marathon meetings to drag on and on.
- Mad-libbing your way through an in-house architecture is also known as "remaking a product in thine own image."
- Are you making it up as you go along? Don't.
- The plane doesn't know who's flying it: technology doesn't care who is pushing the buttons.
- Most of the time in a technical context, the so-called root cause doesn't matter unless you're writing and debugging software. But since you aren't, it doesn't matter at all. However, software issues caused by people, process, and business problems matter a lot.
- You don't need to know if it's corporate sabotage; if it caused unexpected downtime, it's bad. End of story.

- Some questions you ask of me are questions you might as well ask of your Magic 8-Ball. Pay less money for the same service by sending me all the logs I ask for. The first time.
- If it violates the laws of physics…I'll just let you think about that.
- Outsourcing: taking everything that's important and giving it to a stranger (in another country!) is a bad idea.
- Bringing people from another country here is also a bad idea to handle your company's most important data. They are nice, hardworking, intelligent folks, sure. But they are not U.S. Citizens. Is it really worth the gamble? What recourse would you have?
- If you'd be afraid of certain people in a dark alley…Do I need to finish this sentence?

About the Author

S USAN C. COOPER became a technical consultant and architect quite through serendipity more than twenty years ago. Graduating with a BA in English from the University of Texas at San Antonio, she had amassed enough premed classes to apply to medical school (but didn't have the grade point average to get in), and she quickly realized that without a teaching certificate, she would probably starve. So in 1993, during a fairly serious economic depression, she spent a miserable year working as a temp, or secretary, while applying to no less than ten thousand jobs.

How It All Started for Me: In the Author's Words

People at my temp jobs would always ask me how do things on the computer. I was always a little surprised because I didn't really have any special knowledge or training; I would just sit down and figure it out. One day, an IT guy came to work on my PC. I'd probably managed to tweak it a little too much, and I remember being in awe that there was this person walking around, not chained to a desk as I was. Imagine being able to use the bathroom without having to get someone to watch the desk! That person also didn't have someone looking over his shoulder the entire day.

So after a year and a half and hundreds of "Thanks, but no thanks" job application rejections, I got desperate and did two things:

- I moved to Austin, where the economic outlook for skilled workers was brighter.
- In the midst of applying everywhere, I somehow managed to apply for a job with Kelly Services to troubleshoot Windows 95, a new operating system (OS) that hadn't been released yet.

Because it was a new OS, and because we would be trained on it, we were given a basic quiz—ten questions that were easy to answer if you were an IT person but might as well have been in a foreign language for me. Here are two examples:

- How do you print from a DOS prompt?
- How many SCSI devices can be attached to an SCSI controller?

Needless to say, I didn't know the answers, but I did go to Barnes & Noble the next day, having memorized the questions, to look up the answers. Then I showed up at the competing technical agency in town to retake the test. Because Windows 95 was brand-new, the agency was going to teach people they hired the operating system, and I knew with certainty that I could figure it out if I could just get someone to give me a shot, which the competing technical agency did.

Unfortunately, our entire Austin Windows 95 Support Center disbanded just a few months later. I have to assume the agency didn't need our technical support center, which was one of the smallest, but in any case, we were notified of the closure, and about four months later, I was out of a job. I noticed that Kelly Services gave all the men (and our group had been pretty much all men) interviews at some of the big Austin tech firms to support their users on Windows 95—our small support center had had some of the most experienced engineers on this brand-new OS. But what did Kelly Services present me with when I had the same experience as most of the guys? A position as a receptionist at a dental office. I'm not sure if I even bothered to decline it. As an aside, about a year later, one of the recruiters who'd kept an eye on me saw me online and called to see if I was interested in working for them in a technical consulting position. She apologized and said, "You really went out and showed us all. All those guys we hired are still at the same tech companies doing the same level of support." I don't remember the position that I was offered, but at that point, I was earning $200,000 to $250,000 per year as an independent IT consultant in some of the biggest markets in the world.

After the economy failed again in 2001, I picked up a job as a Microsoft Certified Technical Trainer at New Horizons in New Mexico, where I happened to land on the weekends when I would fly home from my job at Merrill Lynch in New York. A couple of years and another ten thousand résumés later (this time, ironically, I was told I was way overqualified), I landed a six-week consulting gig with Microsoft Corporation in the fall of 2003 at FMC Chemical for a new version of a Microsoft product called SMS 2.0.

After spending the past twelve years at Microsoft—working the first decade on our largest enterprise accounts and the last two years in public-sector accounts—I'm now taking a break and finishing up this book, which I started years ago. Prior to working at Microsoft, I ran my own successful S-corporation specializing in systems management consulting—I did this for seven years. I was a partner during that time with both Microsoft Consulting Services (at FMC Chemical in Philadelphia) and Compaq Consulting Services (at Charter Communications in St. Louis and Compaq in Geneva, Switzerland, and Nice, France). I also worked directly with Compaq Computer, Reinsurance Group of America, Charter Communications, Exxon Computing and Network Services, Exxon Pipeline, Merrill Lynch, Premera Blue Cross, USAA, and Lyondell-Citgo.

My extensive experience is almost exclusively with larger enterprise system implementations (seventy thousand to two hundred thousand workstations); server, desktop, and network installation; troubleshooting; and maintenance. The large businesses are not better or worse than small- and medium-sized businesses; that's just where I landed and feel most comfortable. This scale served me well as I transitioned to working with public-sector clients, who, in many cases, dwarf the largest US companies.

Just a note: I do not comment on any public-sector clients at all, ever, in this book. Also, all of my stories have to do with what I learned on my own at the start of my IT career when I worked as a contractor for Fortune 100 companies. And throughout it all, I've enjoyed myself immensely. I wanted to pass along what I've learned. I don't think IT is as difficult as it's made out to be, and I don't think you have to hide behind difficult concepts or technical words. It's in English, for heaven's sake. If someone isn't able to explain something to you simply, it's probably that person who doesn't truly understand it. Bless their heart.